SUPERBASE 18

COLD LAKE

SUPERBASE 18
COLD LAKE

Canada's Northern Guardians

Robbie Shaw

OSPREY
AEROSPACE

Published in 1990 by Osprey Publishing
Limited
59 Grosvenor Street, London W1X 9DA

British Library Cataloguing in Publication
Data

Shaw, Robbie
    Cold Lake. – (Superbase; 18).
    1. Canada. Air bases
    I. Title II. Series
    358.4170971

    ISBN 0-85045-910-9

Editor Tony Holmes
Page design Brenda Burley
Printed in Hong Kong

Acknowledgements

The compilation of this volume would
not have been possible without the
assistance of a number of people at
Cold Lake and the Public Relations
staff at NDHQ in Ottawa. Amongst the
many people at the base who were so
helpful I would like to say a special
thanks to Major Jan Martinsen and
Private Nancy Hamilton of Public
Affairs. Lieutenant Colonel Ian
Struthers, Lieutenant McCutcheon
and Sergeant Cardy Launey of No 441
Sqn and Colonel Lukan at AETE. Also
the photographers of AETE and the
base photographic section deserve a
special mention for providing some
of the excellent shots featured in this
publication.

Front cover Wearing the distinctive
red AETE 'X' on its fin, a typically
grey CAF F/A-18B banks gently over
the picturesque Primose Lake
Evaluation Range. Beneath its wings
are two large 480 gallon fuel tanks
mounted inboard, and a pair of Mk 83
1000 lb bombs on the outer stations
(*AETE*)

Back cover Baring its teeth to the
world, a 23rd Tactical Fighter Wing
(TFW) A-10 Thunderbolt II proves
that the 'Warthog' does indeed have
teeth, especially when it comes to
'tank-busting'

Page two The large Base Aircraft
Maintenance Engineering
Organization (BAMEO) Hangar One
with the control tower located on top
dominates the Cold Lake skyline, and
can be seen from many miles away.

For a catalogue of all books published by Osprey Aerospace
please write to:

**The Marketing Manager, Consumer Catalogue Department
Osprey Publishing Ltd, 59 Grosvenor Street, London, W1X 9DA**

A CF-5A of No 419 'Moose' Sqn in aggressor colours photographed whilst refuelling fom a CC-137 tanker

Introduction

Canadian Forces Base Cold Lake, home of the Canadian fighter pilot, is situated in the remote north eastern corner of Alberta, almost on the border with Saskatchewan. It was opened in 1954 to be used as an air weapons training base, and still performs this vital function today. The base is also home to two frontline squadrons.

Over 3000 military personnel, 3200 dependents and 470 civilian employees live at Cold Lake, making it both the biggest and the busiest fighter base in Canada. Largest resident flying unit is No 419 'Moose' Sqn which operates over 30 CF-5A and B aircraft in the tactical training role. The first of three CF-18 units is No 410 'Cougar' Sqn which acts as the conversion unit, whilst No 416 'Lynx' and No 441 'Silver Fox' Squadrons are operational units. The Base Flight comprises 12 CT-33A 'T-Birds' and three CUH-1H Huey helicopters. Cold Lake is also home to the Aerospace Engineering Test Establishment (AETE), this self-contained unit being responsible for flight testing all aircraft, weapons and avionics systems destined for use in Canadian military aircraft.

The base also looks after the nearby Cold Lake Air Weapons Range (CLAWR), one of the most sophisticated facilities of its type in the world. The range incorporates Cubic ACMI equipment covering 100 target areas with over 700 individual targets ranging from disused vehicles and aircraft to dummy SAM sites and airfields. CLAWR has also been designated a supersonic range, with pilots able to fly their aircraft at speed down to 100 feet. The CLAWR facility is heavily used during the annual Maple Flag exercise which brings together several NATO air forces for six weeks of intensive 'real-life' flying above the Cold Lake pine forests. Basically the Canadian equivalent of the highly successful Red Flag event held at Nellis AFB (featured extensively in Superbase 1), Maple Flag was first held in 1978 and took the form of a twice yearly, four-week long exercise until 1987 when it was rationalized into its current format.

Cold Lake is an extremely modern and well equipped air base with three long runways which handle 140,000 aircraft movements a year. The large Base Aircraft Maintenance Engineering Organization (BAMEO) hangar with the control tower on top dominates the skyline, and this, along with eight other hangars, can accommodate all the aircraft on base – a useful asset during the cold winter months.

One corner of the airfield hosts the Medway Air Terminal to cater for the small number of commercial flights from Edmonton which serve the local towns of Cold Lake, Grand Centre and Medway. The base air traffic controllers also provide a service for flights into seven small regional airports in the area.

Arguably the most important air base in Canada, Cold Lake will continue to play a vital role in the training of NATO forces, as well as CAF fighter crews, well into the next century. Perhaps the base badge, a colourful emblem consisting of three timber wolves looking north, east and west, best represents the vigilance and professional competence of the personnel who function as a team at Cold Lake.

Standing guard over the flags outside Base Headquarters is this CF-101B Voodoo. Although the Voodoo was never based at Cold Lake, the type was a frequent visitor and is remembered with affection by those who were connected with it. Maintained in immaculate condition, this particular aircraft carries the markings of No 410 Sqn on the port side of the fin, and No 416 Sqn on the starboard

Contents

The moose is loose

A trio of CF-5A Freedom Fighters from No 419 'Moose' Tactical Fighter Training Squadron. The CF-5 is officially known in Canada as the CF-116, and No 419 is the largest frontline squadron in Canada with well over 30 aircraft on strength. Formed at RAF Mildenhall in December 1941, No 419 soon acquired its distinctive unit emblem when it adopted the nickname of its first CO, a distinguished aviator by the name of Wing Commander John 'Moose' Fulton (*No 419 Sqn photo*)

No 419 has been the CF-5 Tactical Fighter Training Squadron since 1 November 1975. On completion of basic training on the CT-114 Tutor at CFB Moose Jaw, those destined to be fighter pilots join No 419 to learn how to use the aeroplane as a fighting machine. This includes 175 hours of classroom tuition and 54 hours flying time. The curriculum includes instrument and formation flying by day and night, before proceeding to the low-level and weapons phase of the course. During the latter stages of the course in-flight refuelling from CC-137 tankers is undertaken, again by both day and night. Most of the CF-5As are equipped with bolt-on refuelling probes, though the two-seat CF-5Bs do not have this capability. A student in a CF-5A approaches the 'basket' whilst the instructor alongside in a CF-5B watches and, if necessary, offers advice and encouragement

During the low-level phase of the course pilots are eventually permitted to fly down to heights of only 250 feet, testing their navigational skills at high speed and low altitude over the often featureless terrain of northern Alberta. The squadron's moose insignia is painted on the fin, usually on a pale blue background, as seen on this CF-5A climbing out from a low-level training mission

Below Almost there! The student in this CF-5A inches forward hoping for a successful 'prod'. The art of aerial refuelling is not as easy as it appears. Trying to fly the probe into the drogue basket, which can often oscillate violently in turbulence, requires a smooth approach and immense concentration

Right Most CF-5s are now camouflaged, but some two-seaters retain their natural metal finish

Top and above An important aspect of tactical training is teaching the art of air combat. To make it as realistic as possible the CF-5s are painted up in a variety of camouflage schemes, many of which are similar to those used by USAF aggressor squadrons. In keeping with the spirit of all true aggressor outfits, No 419 adorns their CF-5s with Soviet-style 'bort' numbers

Left Contact! As dusk rapidly approaches this student makes a successful contact with the starboard drogue unit deployed from a CC-137 tanker of No 437 'Husky' Sqn. The rim of the drogue 'basket' contains a traffic light arrangement which is operated by the tanker crew to give instructions to the receiver, thus enabling refuelling operations to be carried out in complete radio silence. The red light tells the pilot of the receiver aircraft not to approach the basket, or, if already 'plugged in', to breakaway immediately. The amber means he is cleared to approach the basket, whilst the green indicates fuel is flowing

The instructor in this CF-5B
approaches the basket to check for
possible damage after an
unsuccessful attempt by one of the
students.

Left Painted up in a new scheme of grey and dark green, with toned down national insignia, this aircraft is being towed back to the No 419 Sqn ramp after engine testing. Parked beyond the CF-18s are a pair of King Air aircraft at the Medway Air Terminal

Above The sheer variety of paint schemes on No 419's CF-5s is clearly visible in this ramp shot of the squadron dispersal. Some of these aircraft are being refuelled between sorties, this mandatory function being performed soon after the pilot has shut down and vacated his mount

Right A CF-5B at rest on a crisp spring morning. Ropes are being used as chocks on this aircraft, standard practice on Canadian fighter bases. The 'Moose' squadron currently has three foreign exchange pilots serving as instructors, one each from France, Germany and the USAF

Above Except for the wingtip tanks this two-seat B model is in clean configuration. Usually No 419 Sqn machines carry weapons pylons or a centreline fuel tank. Air to ground weapons delivery is carried out at the Jimmy Lake Range, whilst air-to-air gunnery is practised against a banner target towed 1500 feet behind another aircraft

Above The squadron's moose insignia on the tail of a CF-5A. Clearly visible is the US style night formation strip light on the fin

Right Amongst the 30 CF-5s on strength with the 'Moose' squadron several have the option of being reconnaissance optimized with the fitment of a detachable nose section which contains three 70 mm Vinten cameras. Originally assigned to the now disbanded No 434 Sqn, these aircraft are designated CF-5ARs when the recce nose is fitted. Tasked with fulfilling the reconnaissance role in a wartime situation, squadron instructors sometimes fly recce equipped aircraft on staff training exercises

116703

Canada

Left In 1989 No 419 Sqn painted an aircraft in a special scheme to commemorate its 25th anniversary (although formed in 1941 the squadron has been disbanded twice) as an active unit. Aircraft No 116703 was the machine chosen, and it frequented a number of airshows in Canada during the summer of 1989

Above A close up of the tail shows the charging moose

Right Three CF-5As overfly the squadron's ramp and hangars (*CAF*)

Above The pilot of this CF-5B holds his hands aloft, clear of the controls and weapons switches, to enable the groundcrew to make a final external check of the aircraft

A CF-5B undergoes a quick check from the groundcrew prior to taxiing for a
training mission

This No 419 Sqn CF-5A is heavily loaded with long range fuel tanks on the inboard pylons and rocket pods on the outboards. Lacking the squadron's moose logo, this machine has only recently been acquired from the AETE, whose 'X' still adorns the aircraft's rudder

Below The first Canadian operator of the CF-5 was the Aerospace Engineering Test Establishment (AETE) at Cold Lake. This unit is tasked with testing all aircraft, associated systems and weapons to be used by the Canadian Forces. The unit still operates a small number of CF-5s, both A and B models, which are frequently used for weapons trials on the nearby Primrose Lake Evaluation Range. This facility is equipped with special targets, tracking radar and photo theodolites. Seen on the Cold Lake ramp, this camouflaged AETE CF-5A is fitted with a special camera pod and extra long pitot tube. Used as the primary weapons platform for CF-5 development flying, this particular aircraft has a white cheat line painted along the length of its fuselage, a device used for photographic reference purposes during test flights (*Tom van Schaik*)

Left All aircraft on strength with the AETE carry a red 'X' for experimental on the fin, as seen on CF-5B 116801. This was the first two-seat CF-5 delivered to the CAF, and has been on AETE strength ever since. Unlike the CF-5As, the B models do not carry any special instrumentation, and are generally used for CF-5 project work, proficiency and chase plane duties. In this photograph the aircraft is carrying a trial acoustic aerial target for air-to-air gunnery work (*AETE*)

The photographers of AETE log almost as much flying time as some of the aircrew as many of the trials conducted have to be photographed from a chase plane, which is usually a CT-33 or CF-5B. This CF-5B was photographed on a chase plane training mission for the benefit of a photographer who had recently joined the AETE (*Peter Foster*)

The AETE is a self-supporting unit and undertakes all servicing of its varied fleet of aircraft, which usually comprises 20 or so airframes of up to eight different types. The unit's pilots will have attended one of the four recognized test pilot schools; the Empire Test Pilots School (ETPS) at Boscombe Down, the Air Force Flight Test Center (AFFTC) at Edwards AFB, the Naval Test Pilot School (NTPS) at NAS Patuxent River or the Ecole du Personnel Navigant D'essais Et De Reception (EPNER) at Istres. Illustrated is CF-5B 116810

Hornet, Canadian style

Identity crisis! This CF-18A Hornet wears the markings of No 410 Sqn, plus the AETE's experimental 'X'. As AETE's three Hornets were heavily involved in other trials the unit borrowed this aircraft for a short term air-to-air refuelling trial with a CC-137 tanker of No 437 'Husky' Sqn (*AETE*)

AETE currently has three CF-18s on strength, including one dual B model. These three are engaged in a full range of projects for the Hornet programme, one of the most recent being to investigate handling characteristics whilst flying with two large 480 gallon underwing fuel tanks, as seen in this shot of the CF-18B. As Cold Lake is located well away from any industrial centres the visibility is generally excellent. Indeed, the limiting factor is usually the range of the human eye (*AETE*)

As the Primrose Lake Range is virtually on Cold Lake's doorstep maximum utilization can be made of aircraft engaged on weapons trials. In this instance, a CF-18B fires a salvo of Canadian designed CRV-7 unguided rockets which are built by Bristol Aerospace. The 'passenger' in the back seat is actually a photographer capturing the event on film for future evaluation. Because many of the test programmes rely on an accurate record of events, a number of systems have been developed to aid the photographers in their demanding tasks. These mainly involve remote controlled still, cine and video cameras mounted externally in strategic places on the aircraft. This particular CF-18 has two cameras attached to a specially adapted missile rail which has in turn been fitted to the starboard wingtip. The AETE CF-18s have been adapted to carry up to 16 cameras on the underside and wingtips, the unit's CF-5s also having a similar capability (*AETE*)

The old and the new. An ageing Canadair CF-104D Starfighter formates with a newly delivered CF-18B equipped with wingtip mounted cameras. The Starfighter has since been retired by the CAF, the AETE being one of the last operators of the classic Lockheed jet. Judging by the lush vegetation below, this shot was taken during the summer (*AETE*)

Left Surrounded by various items of test equipment, and loaded up with a pair of bulky 480 gallon underwing fuel tanks, this AETE CF-18B is parked outside hangar seven at Cold Lake

Above Although No 410 'Cougar' Sqn was the first CAF unit to receive the Hornet in October 1982, the distinction of being the first frontline outfit equipped with the CF-18 went to No 409 'Nighthawk' Sqn. This ex-Voodoo unit began operations with the CF-18 in July 1984 at Cold Lake where it was intended to remain. However, due to structural problems with the twin fin design of the CF-18 deliveries of the aircraft fell behind schedule, whilst in the Federal Republic of Germany the Starfighters of the 1st Canadian Air Group (1 CAG) were being withdrawn from service. To fill the gap in the NATO order of battle the decision was taken to redeploy No 409 to 1 CAG at Baden Soellingen, where it remains today alongside No 421 'Red Indian' and No 439 'Sabre Toothed Tiger' Squadrons. Devoid of external stores, a No 409 Sqn CF-18A performs at an airshow in Europe

Left During the cold winter months at Cold Lake the sun's zenith is rather low, and not at all conducive to good photography. This pair of No 409 Sqn CF-18As were snapped refuelling from a CC-137 over a snow covered Alberta landscape in December 1984

Above The training unit for Canadian CF-18 pilots is No 410 Tactical Fighter (Operational Training) Squadron. The origins of this unit date back to 1941 when it was formed at Ayr, in Scotland, as a night-fighter squadron operating the Boulton-Paul Defiant. Later in the war it flew the Beaufighter and Mosquito before disbanding at the end of hostilities in 1945. It reformed in Canada in 1948 operating the Vampire and soon afterwards the 'Cougars' had the distinction of becoming the first Canadian unit to fly the F-86 Sabre, an aircraft it operated from England and later Germany and France. Subsequently it flew the CF-100 Canuck and CF-101 Voodoo

The CF-18, as it is almost always referred to, is officially known as the CF-188 in Canada, and No 410 Sqn received its first aircraft on 31 October 1982. The squadron devised its own course for students, who graduate from the fighter lead-in course on the CF-5s of No 419 Sqn. This includes 200 hours of ground school, 40 hours simulator time and 85 hours flying. The course curriculum covers learning how to handle the aircraft competently and to its limitations, formation and night flying and using the machine as a weapons platform. Climbing out of Cold Lake's runway 30R in full afterburner is a CF-18B 'twin-sticker' of No 410 Sqn

'Cougar' Sqn CF-18B at rest between missions. The bulbous canopy affords the pilot an excellent view, a definite plus point when it comes to ACM. The dummy canopy painted on the underside of the forward fuselage helps to confuse an adversary as to the aircraft's true aspect during air combat

Above A 'Cougar' Sqn CF-18B armed with rocket pods taxies to the last chance check at the holding point of runway 30R. Being the training unit, No 410 has a large fleet of 27 aircraft, the bulk of which are two-seat B models. The squadron runs two courses per year, each lasting five and a half months and containing 26 students. In addition it is tasked to run Fighter Weapons Instructor (FWI) programmes for all CAF Hornet units; these being the equivalent of a US Navy 'Top Gun' course

Right Number two of a four-ship formation awaits the arrival of his squadron mates prior to a ground attack training mission. To reduce fatigue on the twin fins Hornets have now been fitted with a leading edge extension (LEX) fence, upon which No 410 have painted a running cougar

Left Canadian Hornets retain almost all the features of their US Navy counterparts, including the folding wings displayed by this No 410 Sqn CF-18A. They also retain the catapult launch bar on the nosewheel, as removal of these items would have made the aircraft much more expensive. Another legacy of its carrier lineage are the sturdy main undercarriage legs, ideal for blue water operations

Above Refuelled and rearmed, this CF-18A is almost ready for its next training mission. Long gone are the colourful unit markings of the Voodoo era, replaced by a rather nondescript low visibility grey cougar's head insignia. However, even this was too much for the powers that be and they deemed it was too big. The motif has since been reduced to half size

Overleaf The end of a hard day, and this CF-18B rests in the cool evening air. Although used primarily for training, the two-seat B model is fully operational, and in time of war the instructors and aircraft would be assigned to the NORth American Air Defense Command (NORAD) in the air defence role

Above No 410 Sqn received the 138th, and last, Canadian Hornet on 28 September 1988. The reduced size unit markings and toned down national insignia are illustrated on this late-build CF-18B

Right The final Canadian Hornet unit to form was No 416 Tactical Fighter Squadron, better known as the 'Lynx' squadron. This distinguished unit was formed at Peterhead, in Scotland, on 18 November 1941, and for the next four and a half years flew various marks of Spitfires in England and Europe. Subsequently the squadron operated P-51 Mustangs, then progressed to the jet era and the T-33, F-86, CF-100 and CF-101. No 416 was the last Voodoo air defence squadron, disbanding on 31 December 1984. Nearly four years were to elapse before the 'Lynx' squadron reformed, this time at Cold Lake with the CF-18

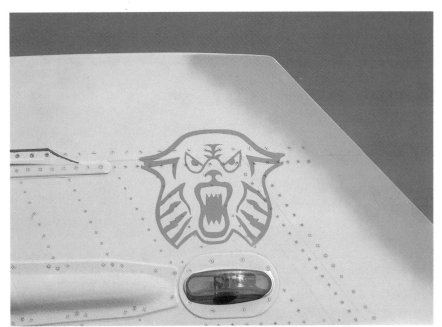

Left The primary role of No 416 Sqn is the rapid reinforcement of NATO's central region, an area to which the unit would deploy with the aid of air-to-air refuelling, operating from CFB Lahr in the Federal Republic of Germany once they had arrived. The unit is supported in this role by No 433 Sqn at Bagotville, Quebec. Illustrated is aircraft No 188798, the last of 98 CF-18As to be delivered to the CAF

Above Unit markings on CAF Hornets are disappointing when compared to those which adorned the Voodoos. The lynx's head on No 416 Sqn aircraft is unrecognizable when viewed at any distance from the aircraft

CFB Bagotville in Quebec is home to two Hornet squadrons; No 425 'Alouette' and No 433 'Porcupine'. The role of the former is air defence whilst the latter is primarily ground attack, with an additional task of NATO reinforcement. Aircraft from these units are not infrequent visitors to Cold Lake where they participate in Maple Flag exercises, or with squadron instructors attending FWI courses. This No 433 Sqn CF-18A is chained down whilst full power ground runs are carried out on the two General Electric F404 engines

A No 433 Sqn CF-18A taxies back to its parking spot whilst participating in the 1989 Maple Flag exercise. The unit previously operated CF-5s before converting to the Hornet in 1988

Above The day's work is over for this 'Porcupine' squadron CF-18A, but it has already been turned around by the maintenance crews ready for the next day's missions. When this photograph was taken 75 per cent of the squadron's aircraft were operating from Cold Lake; seven on Maple Flag and two with the FWI course

Right When full power engine runs are to be carried out it is standard practice for engine guards to be placed in front of the intakes to prevent foreign object damage (FOD). Items such as stones sucked into the engine could damage it irreparably, or even worse the damage might not become apparent until the aircraft is airborne

Above The unit marking carried on the tail of No 433 Sqn Hornets. The small 'e' after 433 stands for Escadron, as the unit is French speaking

Right In keeping with the animal theme that appears to be so popular with CAF Hornet units, the final CF-18 squadron to be found at Cold Lake is No 441 'Silver Fox' Sqn. Formed in Sydney, Nova Scotia, in 1942, the 'Silver Foxes' initially operated Hurricanes before moving across the water to England in 1944 to operate the Spitfire, and later the Mustang. The unit entered the jet era in 1951 with the introduction of the Vampire, before proceeding overseas again with the F-86 Sabre. The introduction of the CF-104 Starfighter saw the unit moved to Lahr, and finally Baden Soellingen where it disbanded in March 1986, thus bringing to an end CAF operations with the venerable Lockheed fighter. It reformed at Cold Lake in June 1987 on the CF-18. Here, one of the unit's female technicians is seen assisting the pilot to strap in

Above The aircraft is given a final 'once over' from the No 441 groundcrew before departing on a transit flight to CFB Comox, British Columbia. The 'Silver Fox' squadron is employed in the air defence role and, as such, is committed to NORAD. Two aircraft maintain an alert facility at Comox from where they can be airborne within minutes of being scrambled to intercept hostile or suspicious contacts. Its sister unit on the east coast is No 425 'Alouette' Sqn at Bagotville, which has an alert facility at Goose Bay. No 441's famous black and white checks have been reduced to low-vis grey, and are now barely visible at the top of the fin

Left Clear to start number two. A 'Silver Fox' Hornet with long range tanks is seen starting up prior to departing on a training exercise. The squadron frequently operates aircraft from forward operating locations (FOLs) such as the civil airfields at Inuvik and Yellowknife in the Northwest Territories, as well as a new facility at Rankin Inlet. Operating from these remote sites with limited facilities in the middle of winter is quite a feat

Left In the warmth of a Cold Lake hangar this 'Silver Fox' jet undergoes systems checks ready for the following day's flying. The luminous strips which assist in night formation flying are clearly visible

Above The Cold Lake 'den' of No 441 'Silver Fox' Sqn

Silver Stars

Right Base Flight's 'T-Birds' all carry the Cold Lake titling in a red and white band on the fin

Far right 1990 saw the Lockheed T-33 Shooting Star trainer celebrate its 42nd birthday, quite a feat for a jet trainer. The Royal Canadian Air Force, as it was then known, took delivery of its first T-33 in 1951. The RCAF eventually received an amazing 656 of these aircraft which were built under license by Canadair in Montreal. Technically designated the CT-133 Silver Star in CAF service, but usually referred to as simply the CT-33A, nearly 70 examples of the venerable trainer still serve with various units. This immaculate looking 'T-Bird' is attached to the AETE where it usually fulfills chase plane and general purpose duties (*AETE*)

Above and right After the CF-5 equipped No 419 Sqn, the CAF's largest unit is
No 414 who fly CT-33s and CC-144s in the ECM role from CFB North Bay. It has
26 'T-Birds' on strength, eight of which are configured as ET-33As, having
underwing pylons to carry chaff dispensing and radar jamming pods. The unit
maintains a large fleet because it is also responsbile for the training of new
CT-33 pilots. One of the main tasks of the squadron is to provide 'silent' targets
for the air defence forces, a role which sees them frequently visiting Cold Lake.
The distinctive black and red rudder markings on this CT-33A denote that it
belongs to No 414 'Black Knights' Squadron

Left For many years CT-33A 133505 has been used by AETE for ejection seat
trials. For this purpose the rear cockpit does not have a canopy, and these days
a dummy is used on ejection trials – a far cry from the days when live
'volunteers' were used. This aircraft was finally withdrawn from AETE use in
mid 1989, and was destined to be stored. It is possible that it may still be used for
ejection seat trials at a later date (*AETE*)

Above Cold Lake's Base Flight is the largest, and has the most diverse task of any Base Flight in Canada. The three CH-118 Huey helicopters are used primarily for rescue and range support work, while the more numerous CT-33A fleet of 12 aircraft performs a variety of tasks, from local weather check flights every morning to towing banner targets for the fighters. The 'T-Bird' is also utilized as a high speed mode of transport for senior officers, as well as acting in the support role for exercises throughout the NORAD region

Left The 'T-Bird' is much loved by CAF pilots, and is so easy and cheap to maintain that it is likely to remain in CAF service into the next century! The Rolls-Royce Nene engine is so reliable and robust that in the words of one CAF technician 'you could throw a rock down the intake and it would spit sand out the jetpipe'. CAF 'T-Birds' are kept in immaculate condition by the technicians, as exemplified by this No 414 Sqn aircraft

Maple Leaf heavy metal

Left above and below Although no longer in CAF service these photographs of the classic Voodoo had to be included. These No 416 'Lynx' Sqn aircraft were participants in the October 1984 Maple Flag exercise, an event which took place just a few months before the last of the CF-101 air defence squadrons disbanded. The Voodoo did, however, put in appearances at Cold Lake after 1984 as No 414 Sqn operated a single EF-101B 'Electric Jet' in the ECM role, and one twin-stick CF-101F, until April 1987

Below A No 416 Sqn CF-101B decelerates with the aid of a brake parachute after landing on runway 30R. The distinctive 'candy striped' control tower is an excellent landmark for crews returning to Cold Lake

A rare photo of a camouflaged Canadian Voodoo of No 416 Sqn. This hastily applied water-based paint helped cut down reflections from the normal gloss grey scheme whilst the unit took part in a Maple Flag exercise

A line-up of Chatham based No 416 Sqn Voodoos at rest between missions. The aircraft nearest the camera has been nicknamed 'Redhot Rhino', a reference to the size of the aircraft's navigator, Captain Hank Dielwart. Rhino hooves on the main undercarriage doors add a further personalized aspect to this Voodoo

Cold Lake oddities

To coincide with the 1989 Maple Flag exercise the base held a rare open day. Needless to say one of the star attractions was the CAF's own air demonstration team, the Snowbirds. In this photograph a Snowbirds pilot's helmet poses on the highly polished wing of one of the team's CT-114 Tutor jets

Above This colourful CT-114 is one of a pair of Tutors belonging to the AETE and is used for proficiency flying and chase plane duties

Right The Canadair CC-144 Challenger is used by No 412 Sqn at CFB Uplands, near Ottawa, as a medium and long range executive transport. These aircraft, which have the range to cross the Atlantic, replaced three CC-117 Falcon 20s, and are frequently used to carry government officials. This Challenger brought the Minister of Defence to Cold Lake for a briefing on the Maple Flag exercise, and to experience a flight in a CF-18

Left As previously mentioned, the CT-33s of No 414 Sqn are frequent visitors to Cold Lake. In addition to being the CT-33 training unit, the squadron was also responsible for providing conversion training onto the CC-117 Falcon 20. When still in frontline service three Falcons were operated by the unit in the ECM role, whilst another three VIP aircraft were on strength with No 412 Sqn. To perform this training task No 414 used one Falcon (117504), which was sometimes flown as a squadron 'hack' to support CT-33 deployments. With the introduction of the CC-144 the Falcons have been withdrawn from service

Below One of the more recent additions to the AETE inventory is this Challenger which has the designation CX-144. It is used as an avionics testbed and, in contrast to the VIP configured CC-144s, is painted in a low visibility grey scheme

Left Like its CT-33s, the three EC-117 Falcon 20s used by No 414 Squadron for ECM training were regular visitors to Cold Lake. These aircraft frequently operated with USAF F-106 and F-15 air defence squadrons assigned to NORAD. The Falcons have now been replaced by an ECM training version of the Challenger

Below left and below Nicknamed 'Pinocchio', this CC-129, better known as the C-47 Dakota, has been a resident at Cold Lake for many years. The reason for the 'nose job' was that the aircraft was equipped with a CF-104 radar to train pilots converting to the fighter in the art of low-level navigation. Until pilots became accustomed to the speed of the Starfighter at low-level, initial training was undertaken on the more cumbersome Dakota. After the CF-104 was retired 'Pinocchio' was transferred to the Base Flight where it was used as a utility transport. It has since been retired, and when photographed in mid 1989 was awaiting allocation of a permanent display area on the base

The AETE rotary fleet consists of two
CH-136 Kiowas and two CH-135 Twin
Hueys, the latter being sometimes
referred to as the CUH-1N

Preserved for posterity

Right As with most bases, Cold Lake has a small collection of historically significant aircraft preserved on display in various spots within its confines. Five aircraft, including the recently retired 'Pinocchio' Dakota, sit outside the base headquarters building. In the foreground of this shot is a Canadair CF-100 Cannuck, nicknamed the 'Clunk' in CAF service, which wears the badge of No 3 (All Weather) Operational Training Unit. Behind the CF-100 is a dual marked CF-101B Voodoo

Below Despite never having been based at Cold Lake, a place has been found for the venerable Voodoo. The base Hornet units, No 410 and No 416 Squadrons, both operated the Voodoo before their present mount, hence the markings which adorn the tail of this aircraft

Prior to the type's retirement, Cold Lake was home to the CF-104 Starfighter
training unit, No 417 Sqn. Therefore, it is hardly surprising that a CF-104 graces
'posterity park' outside base headquarters. The aircraft in question is in fact a
hybrid of two airframes that had been retired, and is in RCAF and Cold Lake
Base Flight markings

Although the type is still in service this CT-133 Silver Star was one of the first candidates for preservation

Maple Flag Phantom IIs

During the 1970s the mighty McDonnell Douglas F-4 Phantom II was the backbone of the USAF's Tactical Air Command and it is not surprising that the type has dominated the Maple Flag ramp over the years. Here, a pair of Seymour-Johnson based F-4Es from the 4th Tactical Fighter Wing's 337th Tactical Fighter Squadron (TFS) get airborne from the 12,600 foot long runway 30R

Above Manoeuvring into its parking slot is an F-4E from the 337th TFS, 4th TFW, a unit which is currently converting on to the F-15E Strike Eagle

Right above and below Air National Guard units also regularly participate in Maple Flag exercises, the skill exhibited by crews on these occasions belying the fact that they are part-time jet jocks. Painted up in European One 'lizard' camouflage, these F-4Ds are from the Georgia Air National Guard's 128th TFS, 116th TFW at Dobbins AFB. The 116th TFW recently transitioned onto the F-15A Eagle

Right The crew of this Air Force Reserve F-4D Phantom did extremely well to bring the aircraft back to Cold Lake after a massive explosion in the starboard engine jetpipe severely damaged the corresponding tailplane. The 'TH' tailcode and Texas flag markings on the fin identify the aircraft as belonging to the 457th TFS, 301st TFW at Carswell AFB

Above Based at Bergstrom in Texas, this RF-4C, captured at rotation point in its take-off run, belongs to the 67th Tactical Reconnaissance Wing (TRW)

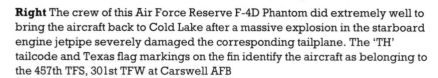

Below The crew of this RF-4C recce bird await taxi instructions before carrying out a pre-strike reconnaissance mission during the Maple Flag XIV exercise. RF-4C units are regular participants in Flag exercises, this machine belonging to the 91st TRS, 67th TRW

Left RF-4C Phantom IIs being prepared for their next mission. The aircraft nearest the camera is being reloaded with chaff and photo flash cartridges

Above The majority of the USAF's Phantom II fleet are now receiving the two tone grey camouflage scheme, as seen on this RF-4C from the Mississippi ANG's 153rd TRS, 186th TRG

Right The camera ports in the nose of this RF-4C are clearly visible

A pair of Mississippi recce RF-4s depart on another sortie. The open doors on the rear fuselage cover the chaff and flash cartridge dispensers

Birds of prey

A line-up of F-15A Eagles from the 49th TFW based at Holloman AFB, New Mexico. Those with yellow fin tips are from the 8th TFS, whilst the blues are from the 7th

Below right An F-15C with the 'FF' tailcode of the 'Fighting First', the 1st TFW based at Langley, Virginia. Members of the 27th TFS are extremely proud of their squadron, hence the appropriately coloured intake and ejection seat covers, the latter complete with squadron emblem

Right A perfect touchdown on runway 12L for this F-15C Eagle. As the runway is long the pilot does not deploy the large airbrake but chooses to keep the nose high for aerodynamic braking instead

Above Maple Flag XXII was the first time the 57th Fighter Weapons Wing (FWW) from Nellis AFB had brought their F-16 Fighting Falcons to Cold Lake. Veterans of many Flag exercises in the venerable F-5E Tiger II, the 57th FWW had only recently completed transitioning onto the F-16 when Maple Flag came around

Above The General Dynamics F-16 Fighting Falcon now dominates the USAF's Tactical Air Command inventory, and as a result the type is becoming a regular sight in the skies over Cold Lake. Loaded with practice bombs, this F-16A from the 63rd Tactical Fighter Training School (TFTS), 56th Tactical Training Wing (TTW) at McDill AFB, Florida, taxies past for an early morning departure during Maple Flag XIV

Above The honour of being the USAF's first F-16 wing belongs to the 388th TFW at Hill AFB, Utah. A component of the wing is the 34th TFS, whose aircraft carry the squadron nickname 'Rams' within their red fin band

The runways at Cold Lake are long enough for F-16s to get airborne safely without the use of afterburner

The majority of F-16 operators previously flew the Phantom II, and the 347th TFW at Moody AFB, Georgia, is no exception. This aircraft from the 68th TFS approaches the holding point of runway 30R, whilst in the background F-15 Eagles prepare to depart from 30L

Strike muscle

Left A typical Maple Flag scene; an FB-111A holds to let a trio of CF-5s taxi back to the ramp, while a pair of Tornados depart in the background

Below An FB-111A from the 509th Bomb Wing (BW) at Pease AFB, New Hampshire, taxies forward from its parking slot at the start of another demanding Flag mission. A member of the groundcrew takes shelter behind the ground power unit to avoid jet blast from the engines

Blast-off! The newly adopted paint scheme on this FB-111A renders the
unit markings virtually invisible from any distance

Right Technicians work to repair a fault on an FB-111A whilst a Base Flight
CH-118 Huey is parked on Search and Rescue standby

Left A low and fast break by a 380th BW FB-111A, despite having the wings swept forward. The FB-111 fleet is currently attached to Strategic Air Command, but the type is soon to be refurbished and reissued to Tactical Air Command as the F-111G

Above right 'Swingers' from the 509th BW on the Cold Lake ramp prepare for their next mission. The aircraft nearest the camera is in the new low visibility scheme with the outline of New Hampshire on the fin, whilst behind is an aircraft in the more traditional FB-111 scheme. In the background is AETE's hangar and some of the unit's varied fleet

Below right Whilst the jets are away the men will play, or in this case sunbathe! FB-111 groundcrews enjoy the summer sunshine whilst awaiting the return of their swing-wing bombers from a Flag mission

Above In stark contrast to the sleek lines of the Eagles, Falcons and Hornets that seem to proliferate at Cold Lake this fearsome looking A-10A Thunderbolt II gives off a far more pugnacious air. Deployed to Canada on a 'tank-busting' exercise, this aircraft, along with others from the 23rd TFW at England AFB, Louisiana, spent many hours over the nearby Fort Wainwright ranges working closely with CAF ground units

Left The size of the large BAMEO hangar is readily apparent, even though only half of it is visible in this shot

European flavour

Right and below Exercises such as Maple and Red Flag provide ideal training for operators in the E-3 AWACS aircraft. These gatherings are amongst the few occasions when large multi-role, multi-national formations can be directed by the 'airborne eyes'. Crews from both the USAF's 552nd Airborne Early Warning & Control Wing (AW & CW) at Tinker AFB, Oklahoma, and the NATO AEW Force at Geilenkirchen Luxembourg, participate on an alternating weekly or fortnightly basis. The NATO Force usually bring a back-up aircraft which, due to lack of space at Cold Lake, will reside at CFB Namao, Edmonton. In this view a NATO E-3A Sentry departs Cold Lake

Above The eyes of the AWACS – a close up of the large radome which houses the Westinghouse AN/APY-1 surveillance radar. The NATO Airborne Early Warning Force comprises eighteen aircraft, with multi-national crews from the NATO countries

Right Units from Royal Air Force Germany (RAFG) have frequently taken part in Maple Flag. During the 1989 Flag, Tornados took part for the second phase of the exercise, the aircraft deploying from Goose Bay where they were located for low level training. RAFG maintains a permanent detachment at Goose during the summer months, where it deploys a mix of aircraft from all RAFG units, with the air and ground crews changing over periodically. This No 9 Sqn Tornado GR.1 is manned by a crew from No 20 Sqn

Above With Skyshadow ECM pods on the outboard pylons, a Tornado prepares to depart on a mixed attack mission with USAF F-16s. Although devoid of unit markings due to a recent service and respray, this aircraft actually belongs to No 20 Sqn, based at RAFG Laarbruch

Right No 16 Sqn Tornado lifts off into the murky overcast skies. British crews feel quite at home in such conditions as they frequently prevail in the UK and northern Germany

Previous pages Between missions the groundcrews scurry around the aircraft like ants, refuelling and preparing it for the next sortie

441

CANADA
MAPLE
FLAG
CFB COLD LAKE

410
COUGARS

CANADIAN FORCES BASE
COLD LAKE

CANADA
HORNET